U.S. Coast Guard Cutters

Carrie A. Braulick
AR B.L.: 3.6
Points: 0.5   MG

MILITARY VEHICLES

U.S. COAST GUARD CUTTERS

by Carrie A. Braulick

Reading Consultant:
Barbara J. Fox
Reading Specialist
North Carolina State University

Capstone

Mankato, Minnesota

Blazers is published by Capstone Press,
151 Good Counsel Drive, P.O. Box 669, Mankato, Minnesota 56002.
www.capstonepress.com

Library of Congress Cataloging-in-Publication Data
Braulick, Carrie A., 1975–
    U.S. Coast Guard cutters / by Carrie A. Braulick.
    p. cm.—(Blazers. Military vehicles)
    Summary: "Describes cutters, their design, equipment, weapons, and role in
the U.S. Coast Guard"—Provided by publisher.
    Includes bibliographical references and index.
    ISBN-13: 978-0-7368-6455-8 (hardcover)
    ISBN-10: 0-7368-6455-5 (hardcover)
    1. Revenue cutters—United States—Juvenile literature. 2. United States.
Coast Guard—Juvenile literature. I. Title. II. Series.
VM397.S76 2007
623.826'3—dc22
                                                 2006002571

Editorial Credits

Martha E. H. Rustad, editor; Thomas Emery, designer; Jo Miller,
    photo researcher/photo editor

Photo Credits

AP/Wide World Photos/Stuart Ramson, 21 (top)
Check Six/George Hall, 4–5; Sam Sargent, 10–11 (top)
Code Red/Barry Smith, 16–17
DVIC/TSGT Steve Faulisi, USAF, 18
Photo by Ted Carlson/Fotodynamics, 10 (bottom), 22–23, 28–29
U.S. Coast Guard Photo/PA1 Danielle DeMarino, 6; PA1 John Gaffney, 21
    (bottom); PA1 Telfair H. Brown, 15; PA2 Andrew Shinn, 7 (top); PA2
    Donnie Brzuska, 7 (bottom); PA2 NyxoLyno Cangemi, 26; PA3 Bobby
    Nash, 20; PA3 Bridget Hieronymus, 19, 27; PA3 Dana Warr, 14; PA3 Mike
    Lutz, cover, 8-9; PAC Jeff Hall, 13 (top); Rob Rothway, 13 (bottom)
U.S. Navy Photo/J01 Dave Fliesen, 24–25

1 2 3 4 5 6 11 10 09 08 07 06

TABLE OF CONTENTS

COAST GUARD CUTTERS

Seeing a Coast Guard cutter can fill a person with joy or fear. People who need to be rescued are happy to see a cutter. But criminals who see a cutter know they are in trouble.

U.S. COAST GUARD

720

When duty calls, cutters answer.
Cutter crews do search-and-rescue
missions. They also clear icy waterways
and stop people who break laws.

DESIGN

Not all Coast Guard boats are cutters. Cutters are at least 65 feet (20 meters) long. They carry supplies so crews can live on the ships.

717

COAST GUARD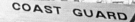

MEDIUM ENDURANCE CUTTER

★ ★ ★ ★ ★ ★

High and Medium Endurance cutters patrol in deep ocean areas. Helicopters take off from and land on these huge ships.

BLAZER FACT

When the Coast Guard began in 1790, it had only 10 cutters. Now, the Coast Guard uses more than 200 cutters.

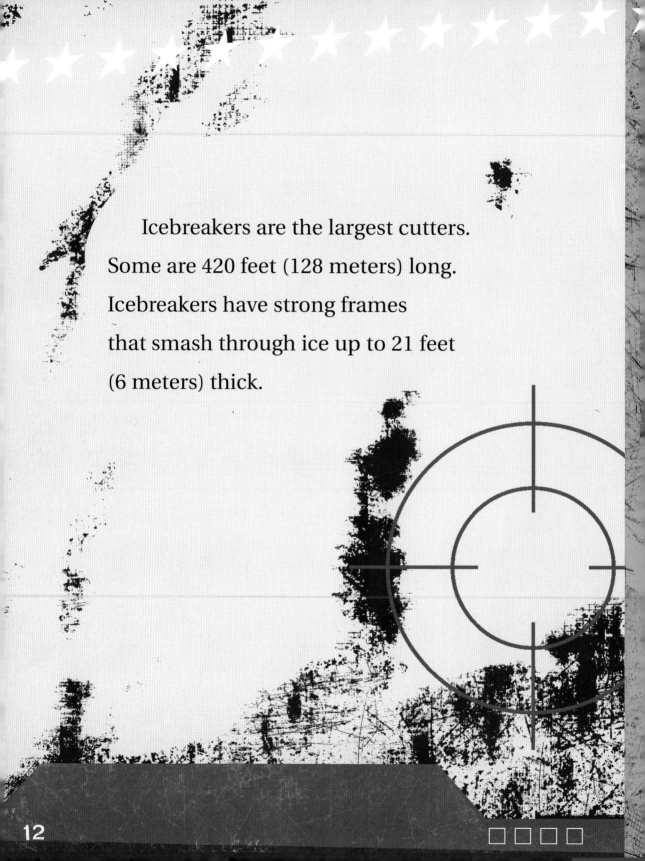

Icebreakers are the largest cutters. Some are 420 feet (128 meters) long. Icebreakers have strong frames that smash through ice up to 21 feet (6 meters) thick.

The Mackinaw icebreaker works in the Great Lakes. It keeps waterways open during winter.

U.S. COAST GUARD 83

PATROL BOAT

The smallest cutters cruise near coasts and on rivers. These patrol boats are about 100 feet (30 meters) long. Their small size helps them pick up speed quickly.

U. S. COAST GUARD

204

BLAZER FACT

Cutters called buoy tenders help the Coast Guard care for its system of floating markers, or buoys.

WEAPONS AND EQUIPMENT

Cutters carry a lot of rescue equipment. Crews unload rigid hull inflatable boats to make rescues during storms.

RIGID HULL INFLATABLE BOAT

Cutter crews control the ship from the bridge. Crews watch radar screens to scan the sky and water for other ships and planes. They can communicate with crews on other ships by radio.

Anyone who dares to fight a cutter is in trouble. Cutters have powerful guns. The mighty Mark 75 machine gun fires bullets into targets at sea or in the air.

BLAZER FACT

The Mark 75 machine gun can fire 80 bullets per minute.

.25-CALIBER GUN

.50-CALIBER GUN

CUTTER DIAGRAM

BRIDGE

MARK 75 GUN

U. S.

HULL

904

RADAR ANTENNA

LANDING PAD

COAST GUARD

904

ABOARD CUTTERS

About 100 people live and work on the largest cutters. In addition to rescues and patrols, their jobs include fixing the ship, running the ship's computers, and making meals.

Crews may spend months at a time on a cutter. They eat in mess decks and sleep in small bunks. Day after day, cutter crews patrol the seas to keep the United States and the oceans around it safe.

MESS DECK

BUNK

HEADING OUT TO SEA!

87347

GLOSSARY

bridge (BRIJ)—the control center of a ship

bullet (BUL-it)—a small, pointed metal object fired from a gun

buoy (BOO-ee)—a floating marker in the ocean

criminal (KRIM-uh-nuhl)—someone who commits a crime

mission (MISH-uhn)—a military task

patrol (puh-TROIIL)—protecting or keeping watch over something

target (TAR-git)—an object that is aimed at or shot at

READ MORE

Demarest, Chris L. *Mayday! Mayday!: A Coast Guard Rescue.* New York: Margaret K. McElderry Books, 2004.

Lurch, Bruno. *United States Coast Guard.* U.S. Armed Forces. Chicago: Heinemann, 2004.

Stone, Lynn M. *Coast Guard Cutters.* Fighting Forces on the Sea. Vero Beach, Fla.: Rourke, 2006.

INTERNET SITES

FactHound offers a safe, fun way to find Internet sites related to this book. All of the sites on FactHound have been researched by our staff.

Here's how:

1. Visit *www.facthound.com*

2. Choose your grade level.

3. Type in this book ID **0736864555** for age-appropriate sites. You may also browse subjects by clicking on letters, or by clicking on pictures and words.

4. Click on the **Fetch It** button.

FactHound will fetch the best sites for you!

INDEX